山有蕨薇
向日葵中英雙語短詩選

My Twitter Tiny Little Poems
Special Bilingual Edition

Christine Yunn-Yu Sun

山有蕨薇 / My Twitter Tiny Little Poems

這本中英雙語短詩選乃專門為付費讀者製作。
請尊重作者權益，切勿修改、複製、刪節、轉寄或轉售其內容，
以免觸犯著作權法。
This bilingual book is copyright. Except for private study, research,
criticism or review, as permitted under the Copyright Act,
no part of this book may be reproduced, stored in a retrieval system,
or transmitted in any form by any means without proper written permission.
Enquiries should be made to the publisher.

《山有蕨薇：向日葵中英雙語短詩選》
作者：向日葵
My Twitter Tiny Little Poems: Special Bilingual Edition
By Christine Yunn-Yu Sun

首版於 2015 年，第二版於 2018 年由電書朝代製作發行，推廣銷售
電書朝代為澳洲 Solid Software Pty Ltd 經營擁有
First published in 2015. This edition published in 2018
by eBook Dynasty, an imprint of Solid Software Pty Ltd.
P.O. Box 218, Belgrave, Victoria 3160, Australia
Web: www.ebookdynasty.net   Email: contact@ebookdynasty.net
"Independence in Writing, Freedom in Publishing."

山有蕨薇 / My Twitter Tiny Little Poems

給　我的家人
他們讓我記得
愛就是詩

For My Family
who helps me remember:
Love is Poetry

目錄 / Index

本書介紹 / Introduction	6
關於「山有蕨薇」/ A Note on the Chinese Title	8
思念 / Missing You	12
良人 / For Leslie	14
翻譯 / Translation	16
回憶 / Farewell	18
母親 / Motherhood	20
回聲 / Echo	22
錯誤 / Mistake	24
洋蔥 / Onion	26
善意 / Keep It White	28
學位 / PhD	30
半月 / Half Dome	32
越界 / Border Crossing	34
痴迷 / Addiction	36
無名 / Soldier	38
比較 / Competition	40
流浪 / Homeless	42
囚犯 / Prisoner	44
判斷 / For Oskar	46
寫作 / Writing	48
穿越 / Traveller	50

山有蕨薇 / My Twitter Tiny Little Poems

鬼魂 / Ghost	52
奇人 / The Doctor	54
標本 / Specimen	56
作者 / Author	58
精讀 / Reading	60
幸福 / Happiness	62
處決 / Execution	64
愛情 / Love	66
追求 / Pursuit	68
約會 / Date	70
卷末語 / Author's Note	74
關於作者 / About This Author	80

本書介紹

這本小書裡收錄的三十首短詩都是在 2015 年四月創作的。詩歌不是我擅長的文類，但是這次碰到「全國詩歌月」(National Poetry Writing Month, or NaPoWriMo) 的挑戰，和許多網路文友的鼓勵，不禁躍躍欲試，寫出來的作品優劣不齊，還請各家指點。

這些短詩原本以英文發表在社交媒體推特 (Twitter) 上，如今在集結成書的時候才翻譯成中文，全書得以雙語形式呈現。眾所周知，推特的發文只限一百四十個字元 (character)，每次還得加入 hashtag — #NaPoWriMo 以及 #tinylittlepoem — 註明是為全國詩歌月所寫的短詩，能用的空間實在有限。然而這種字數限制卻意外地開啟了無限的想像空間，精鍊了文字，卻是當初始料未及。在翻譯方面，一百四十個中文字足夠寫論文了，但為了保持短詩的原味，用字當然要儘量儉省，也不必逐字逐句詮釋，反而像是一種再創作。

山有蕨薇 / My Twitter Tiny Little Poems

Introduction

The 30 tiny little poems collected in this book were written in April 2015, for the National Poetry Writing Month (NaPoWriMo) challenge. Poetry is not a genre I truly understand. However, thanks to the kind support from a wide range of friends online, I dared to give it a go. Your comments on how these poems may be improved will be gratefully appreciated.

  These poems were first published on Twitter, which requires each Tweet to be 140 characters or less. The available space is in fact even less, due to the need to use the hashtags #NaPoWriMo and #tinylittlepoem. Interestingly, I have found such limitation helps tremendously to inspire me and fine-tune my use of words, which ix extremely rewarding. One more note: The Chinese translation was done long after the English poems were written, when the decision to gather them as a book was made. As a result, it is more like re-writing in a different language, instead of word-by-word conversion from one to the other.

關於「山有蕨薇」

眾所周知,「山有蕨薇」一詞出於《詩經・小雅》的〈四月〉,一首感嘆流放困頓的政治諷喻詩。當初為了「四月」而想到這首詩,因為古往今來的無數文人已經把「天若有情天亦老」這個至美的詩句用到浮濫(著名的配句包括「月如無恨月長圓」和「人間正道是滄桑」),如今當然也不能用「四月有情」當作書名,以免褻瀆了多位民初文人的浪漫傳奇。

想來想去,發現「山有蕨薇」這句話很適合自己現今的居住環境,也可比喻文思蓬勃,「四月」更是現成的,便拿來用了。後來深思,像我這樣在兩種語言和文化之間輾轉往復,大概也有點放逐的意思吧。

山有蕨薇 / My Twitter Tiny Little Poems

A Note on the Chinese Title

"Even the gods would grow old if they knew what Love is" -- this notion was first proposed in Chinese literature by a poet in the eighth century. Since then, numerous Chinese poets have written about Love and its impact on both heaven and earth. Yet it was only in recent years that the concept was famously connected with the month April in a Taiwanese television series exploring the complex nature of love affairs among a group of Chinese writers and poets in the beginning of the 20th century.

    The Chinese title of this book depicts the lush ferns growing deep in a mountain. It comes from the poem "April" in the *Book of Songs*, a classic Chinese collection of court hymns and folk songs gathered between the 11th and 7th centuries BC. The poem describes the hardships one suffers in exile, but the reference of ferns gives a hint of everlasting hope. Having composed my tiny little poems in English in April, many of which are about love found and/or lost, and now, having re-interpreted these poems in Chinese -- I suppose it is only natural that feelings of wandering between languages and cultures have arisen.

山有蕨薇 / My Twitter Tiny Little Poems

詩是唯一的所在
讓人們能透露其初始的性靈。
詩是宣洩的出口,
讓人們在公開場合分享
私底下的感知。

～美國詩人艾倫・金斯堡

山有蕨薇 / My Twitter Tiny Little Poems

Poetry is the one place
where people can speak their original human mind.
It is the outlet
for people to say in public
what is known in private.

~ Allen Ginsberg

思念

想你,我是一枝無墨的筆,
走過無數書頁,
尋不到文字或圖畫。
來寫我吧。

山有蕨薇 / My Twitter Tiny Little Poems

Missing You

Missing you, I am an ink-less pen,
drifting through book
without a word or image.
Come write me.

良人

愛了你十二年，
一段終止的旋律，一頁闔上的書，
一個古老傳說的回音。

山有蕨薇 / My Twitter Tiny Little Poems

For Leslie

For twelve years I loved you,
a silenced melody, a page burned black,
echo of an ancient tale.

翻譯

　　一字一槳,我划入
　　星塵滿佈的銀河,
　　沐浴在無止盡的愛情裡。

山有蕨薇 / My Twitter Tiny Little Poems

Translation

Word by word, I paddle into
this dream, a galaxy of bliss,
an oasis of love without end.

回憶

直達過去的火車月台佈告：
「全線關閉，今日停駛。」
我只能改天再想念你。

山有蕨薇 / My Twitter Tiny Little Poems

Farewell

Down that memory lane, road sign:
"Wrong Way – Go Back."
I never saw you again.

母親

能出版一本空白的書，
幫它自己寫出
曠世巨作，
實在是一種榮幸。

山有蕨薇 / My Twitter Tiny Little Poems

Motherhood

It is an honour
to publish a book of blank pages
and help it to write itself
into a masterpiece.

回聲

為何呼喚我，
在你離去之後？
等待、回應著虛空，
潘朵拉之盒中僅剩的罪惡
便是期盼。

Echo

Why call me
after you are gone?
Responding to a void, waiting,
the only evil remaining in my box
is hope.

錯誤

失足離開了你，
無法再回頭。
夜晚，我聽見群星
閃爍著淚水。
你是我的故鄉。

Mistake

I can never go back,
having fallen from you.
At night, I hear the stars
blinking their tears.
You were my home.

洋蔥

甘願為你哭，
把心切成千萬片，
縱然你不喜它，
只愛它的佐味。

山有蕨薇 / My Twitter Tiny Little Poems

Onion

Happy to cry to you,
tearing my heart into pieces,
even though you love not it,
only its flavour.

善意

騙我，
好讓我愛上你。
沒有晴天的預報
我受不了陰雨。
城市沒有公園和鴿群
沒有紅綠燈
就沒有生命。所以
騙我吧，
好讓我繼續前行。

山有蕨薇 / My Twitter Tiny Little Poems

Keep It White

Lie to me
so I will love you.
Without a forecast of sunshine
I cannot bear the storm.
A city without parks and pigeons
and traffic lights
is dead. So
lie to me
to keep me beeping.

學位

當我的論文大功告成，
你便成為一個註釋。
引用過你太多次，
如今一頁頁把你刪除。
我已經建立新的研究框架，
轉而探索其他假設。
此後你只是一個曾經，
文獻綜論裡的一段描述。

山有蕨薇 / My Twitter Tiny Little Poems

PhD

When you became an endnote,
my thesis was done.
Quoted enough from you,
without a mention in every page.
My paradigm had shifted,
exploring a brand new hypothesis.
Now you would only remain
part of my literary review.

半月

妳古老的臉
滿是淚痕　和
旅人們夢想的污漬，
耳後是
初生的太陽。

山有蕨薇 / My Twitter Tiny Little Poems

Half Dome

That ancient face of yours,
tear-stricken, smudged with
travellers and dreams,
I see sunrise
behind your ears.

越界

移民回來伴著妳,
為了愛情,
我的肉體卻留在
夢鄉裡
和她廝守。

Border Crossing

I migrated back to you
with love,
but my body remains
in dreams
with him.

痴迷

我如何能放棄妳
如雨的言詞
澆灌著無分行頁的天空
誘惑著我的筆。

Addiction

How can I give you up,
your rainbow of words
dancing across the page-less sky,
baiting my pen.

無名

留我在這裡
伴野花成長。
異鄉的土壤甜而靜謐,
讓我想起母親。
多年之後我的枯骨
詩篇般散落無蹤,
我的歌卻依然清亮,
在煦日下燦爛發光。

註:紀念第一次世界大戰中死於法國的一位澳洲士兵。

山有蕨薇 / My Twitter Tiny Little Poems

Soldier

Leave me here
to push up flowers.
Foreign soil, sweet and quiet,
reminds me of Mother.
Years later my bones
are scattered like poems,
yet my song is found
blooming under the sun.

* Thanks to: Private Norman Eric Beard, who was killed in action at Boursles, France, on April 6, 1917. He was 24 and has no known grave. For details of his story, please see "Postcard inspires historian's hunt for Oatlands' lost soldiers"
(http://www.themercury.com.au/news/tasmania/postcard-inspires-historians-hunt-for-oatlands-lost-soldiers/story-fnj4f7k1-1227300075195)

比較

如何才能說服你
我其實比她好？
儘管去愛她
而沒有多少回報，
或者選擇我
全心為你存在的靈魂？
浸淫於她的笑貌，你可以
品嚐她唇邊美酒。
我只能和你共患難，
飲你這苦杯，爬你這天梯。

乘她的翅翼翱翔吧。
隨風逐流的時候，請記得：
我的田園等著你
攜手播種，同生偕老。

山有蕨薇 / My Twitter Tiny Little Poems

Competition

How should I convince you
I am better than her?
Love her all you want
yet receive less,
or choose me when you can
in return with my soul?
Drink her smile, you may
taste her lips of wine.
It is me who cry with you,
my bitter cup, my crawl.

Take her wings and fly.
While drifting, remember:
my garden is ready
to plant our trees and grow.

流浪

他要的只是一個地方
讓心歸宿,
一片永恆的綠園
讓他種下希望
看它成長。

Homeless

All he wants is a place
for his heart to be,
a patch forever green
where he can grow hope
and watch it grow.

囚犯

你朦朧的心
阻斷我的自由之路。
我渴望海浪，孤舟
遠離這迷天霧地的海岸。
孤堡裡的狼群在嘶嚎，
詛咒我的靈魂，浸冷我的骨血。
牠們和我一樣顫抖：
你的半月是否會圓？

山有蕨薇 / My Twitter Tiny Little Poems

Prisoner

Your opaque heart
blinds my path to freedom.
I long for the waves, a raft
away from your misty shore.
Wolves in my castle, they howl,
a soul-cursing sound, a chill.
Like me, they tremble:
Will your half moon be full?

判斷

或許妳找到了真愛，
有如一隻春蠶
在半蝕葉片的邊緣窺伺，
或是蒼白的海濤載著漁船
絕望地撞上斷裂的海岸；
或是公園裡的一張空椅
在摧毀世界的風暴中濕透，
或是一盞眨眼的紅燈
夢想所有的交通靜止。

時間繼續在走，夜鷹嚎啼，
因為妳找到了真愛。
又或許妳沒有：
否則夜幕為何要降臨
探觸妳顫抖哭泣的心。
如果妳不確定，那就
拉開眼前的窗簾：
窗上的敲擊開始時，
請妳愛的那人進來。

山有蕨薇 / My Twitter Tiny Little Poems

For Oskar

Perhaps you have found love,
like a silkworm peeking
over the edge of her half-gnawed leaf,
or a pale wave crashing, carrying boats,
hopelessly onto the broken shore;
or a park bench soaking, in storm
that drives the world to silence,
or a red light blinking, dreaming
all the traffic stopping dead.

The clock keeps ticking, owls hooting,
because you have found love,
Or, perhaps you have not,
for the night comes probing
your quivering, crying heart.
Should you be suspicious, then
pull back the curtains for sure:
When the knocking on window begins,
only invite the right one in.

寫作

你尋找著午夜，
爬過蒼白的沙漠，
把沙土變成星辰。
你的女人從綠洲來，
雙眼閃爍睡夢的渴求，
你卻不愛她。
耳邊傳來一聲槍響，
你嚇得坐直身子，回到原點。
眼前是冷血的一片空白，
等你再度啟程
向設定的黎明前進。

山有蕨薇 / My Twitter Tiny Little Poems

Writing

Searching for Midnight,
you crawled across the pale desert,
turning dust to stars.
Out of that oasis came your girl,
her eyes shining with dreams,
yet you desired not her.
A cold gunshot rang through the air,
you jolted awake, finally home.
Staring at you was that blank page,
calling you on to another journey
toward the keyboarded dawn.

穿越

宇宙的另一端
是我的時光機器。
她的一吻顛倒沙漏,
把我狂喜的年少
變幻成迷失灰暗的陰影。
我努力尋覓,把
夢想射入蒼芎。
眼前卻只有她的擁抱
永恆環繞著行星,
我永遠比不上的一尊磐石。

山有蕨薇 / My Twitter Tiny Little Poems

Traveller

On the other side of the universe
is my time machine.
Her kiss turns the hourglass,
turning my youthful bliss
into a shadow lost and grey.
Trying to find her, I
launch my dream into space.
All I see is her fresh embrace
forever around a planet,
a rock I can never be.

鬼魂

他們說妳已經消逝,
我卻感知妳的存在,
陰影竄過我的血液
驅使我發狂冰涼。
我如何能沒有妳
潛伏在紙頁中
操控我的筆四處遊蕩?
我自動書寫:
「I HERE」——這並非我的話
而是妳的,藍色血液
從中間三個字母滴落。
因而我察覺妳的愛
至死不休——永遠
夢想,渴望,尋覓。

山有蕨薇 / My Twitter Tiny Little Poems

Ghost

They say you exist no more,
but I feel your presence,
your shadow in my veins
driving me mad and cold.
What would I do without you
lurking over the pages,
commanding my pen to wander?
Automatically I write:
"I HERE" - it is not my voice
but yours, blue blood dripping
down the middle three letters.
Thus I sense your love
beyond grave – an eternity
of dreaming, longing, searching.

奇人

兩顆心跳動的聲音
是一扇空白鏡面。
連她消逝的幽魂都無法
填補這片虛無,
往日的歡樂早已成空。
孤獨的天使,你受詛咒
只能是永遠的路人,
看他們識對識錯,
讓他們大起大落。
他們的命運就是殘酷
對待你滴血的溫柔靈魂。

山有蕨薇 / My Twitter Tiny Little Poems

The Doctor

The sound of two hearts beating
is an empty mirror.
Not even her faded ghost
lasts, in this void
where joy used to rest.
My Lord, a lone angel, cursed
to forever pass by,
to glimpse their black or white,
to let them stand and fall.
It is their destiny to be cruel
to your tender, bleeding soul.

標本

我的心抽空了你：
沒有靈，沒有歌，沒有陰影
在這鏡面，只是一片靜海。
晶體化的水底
是我解剖針穿的人生，
罕見而纖細，殼下的翅翼
依然想飛。

Specimen

My mind is empty of you:
No soul, no song, no shadow
in my mirror, a silent sea.
Under this crystallised water
is my life dissected and pinned,
rare and fine, shell shining,
still eager to fly.

作者

就為一個名字，我發現了妳——
從此必須學著愛妳，
這倒無妨——故事的開頭
值得所有情節。
妳眨眨眼睛，回頭
愛上了我——
有如雨水滋潤大地，
種子打著呵欠甦醒，
伸個懶腰便是綠意。
我心慌意亂，在人生的書中
急著尋找另一個名字，
就此逃離。妳成了真——
我要的只是一個名字。

山有蕨薇 / My Twitter Tiny Little Poems

Author

Once upon a name, I found you –
Had to learn to love you,
but that was fine – the bud
was well worth the petals.
Slowly you blinked twice
and loved me in return –
like rain caressing the land,
awakening a seed, who yawned
and gave birth to a leaf.
Unnerved, in my book of life,
searching for the next name,
I fled. You became real –
but a story only your name was.

精讀

　　她是一本好書——
　　文字如剃刀尖銳，
　　讓你的靈魂淌空。
　　你要謹慎地選擇，因為
　　這本書給你的記憶
　　留下傷疤，讓你的
　　瞎眼只看見死亡
　　永遠被千百頁文字凌遲——
　　再好不過的一個故事。

山有蕨薇 / My Twitter Tiny Little Poems

Reading

She is a good read –
with love sharp as razor
to bleed out your soul.
Exercise caution when browsing,
for this title scars forever
your memory, blinding you
with a vision of death
by a thousand paper cuts –
an excellent story.

幸福

寂靜。咖啡。餅乾。
寫字。閱讀。夢想。
鍵盤。螢幕。檯燈。
作家在創造世界。

山有蕨薇 / My Twitter Tiny Little Poems

Happiness

Silence. Coffee. Biscuit.
Writing. Reading. Daydreaming.
Keyboard. Screen. Lamp.
A writer at work.

處決

你死於騷亂，
當所有承諾只是
謀殺的暗刀，
當失落只是
貪婪豪求的捷徑，
當辯論變得廉價，
從昂貴的口唇滾落，
當眼淚失去真實，
偽裝著獰笑與自豪。
你死得徒然，
為獅群眼中
比罪惡更惡的罪惡
付出代價。
你問，什麼是公義，
如果羊群中黑白交雜，
一人的良知
竟然是他人的藉口。
你哭著死去，
以為你完全孤獨，
然而你依然希望
有朝一日重見光明。

Execution

You died in chaos,

when promises were knives

stabbing you in the back,

when your loss was used

as shortcut for personal gain,

when words were cheap,

voiced by expensive lips,

when tears were fake,

disguising a sneering pride.

You died in vain,

paying for your wrong

that is wronger than it is

in the eyes of lions.

Then what is right, you ask,

when one's humble conscience

becomes another's excuse

in a mixed mob of sheep.

You died in tears,

thinking you were alone,

but you died in hope

that there one day would be light.

愛情

妳為誰而受傷?
妳拭去血滴,
它卻流淌不停。

山有蕨薇 / My Twitter Tiny Little Poems

Love

Who are you hurt for?
You wipe off the blood,
but it keeps dripping.

追求

追逐那遙遠的夢:
妳微笑的蛆洞中
是否有星光閃耀?
我終究能擁抱妳,
感受妳的重力,
輕觸妳的姿色?
抑或要繼續等待,
永遠在塵世看著殘日
崩潰於空無之中?
也許我應該放棄,
痴心相信遙遠的軌道
不可能有彩虹?
我如何能安睡,
明知妳的裊裊回音
響徹黑暗的雲端?
我往復奔走,迴繞
妳溫柔的眼睛,期盼
生命終將復甦:
妳的眼睛——無休止的暗紅,
笑看昨日明日的彗星,
呼喚他們歸來。

山有蕨薇 / My Twitter Tiny Little Poems

Pursuit

Chasing that distant dream:
In your smiling worm hole,
is that a star swinging?
Will I ever get there
to feel your gravity, to
taste and touch your colour?
Or should I wait on earth
forever, until the sun sets
over event horizon?
Perhaps I should give up,
abandon hope for a rainbow
arching across the orbit.
But how can I rest,
with your echo ringing,
penetrating the darkness?
I am near and far, circling
around you eye, lovingly,
waiting for life to emerge.
Your eye - that ceaseless crimson,
winking at a comet or two,
calling them home.

約會

我準備自己面對生命的終結：
親愛的，和你的這次約會
值得犧牲所有的血肉。
我渴望你的吻，玫瑰般溫柔，
愛撫我如風過林梢，
舒緩我貞潔的天色。
我迎向你的目光，羞怯地
解衣般卸下所有戒備，
邀請你狂放的入侵。
你喃喃的低語似雪冰涼犀利，
我的心撕碎、淌血，
為你留下銀色的印痕。
我愉悅地嘶喊，深知你
無窮的力道足以延續至永遠，
你的強健勇猛讓我瘋狂！
在那之後，我疲倦地躺著，
慢慢墜入無夢的夜眠，
而你到了早上就會離去。
我只有你溫馨的回憶，輕嘆著
挺身迎接另一個愛人，
又一本讓人歡喜讚嘆的好書。

Date

I prepare myself for life's end:
A date with you, my dear,
is worth all the flesh and blood.
I long for your kiss, tender as rose,
caressing like breeze through the bush,
darkening my pink-blue sky.
Desiring your gaze, shyly,
I shed all caution like a dress,
inviting your merciless attack.
Your words are sharp, cold as ice,
cutting, bleeding my heart, leaving
silver marks in my mind.
I cry out in bliss, knowing you
can and will last forever,
your strength, that thrilling power!
Then, when all is done, exhausted,
I drift into a dreamless sleep,
knowing by morning you will be gone.
With your loving memory, I sigh
and reach for a fresh lover,
a brand new book of wonder and awe.

山有蕨薇 / My Twitter Tiny Little Poems

　　　詩是回聲，
　　邀請影子的共舞。

～美國詩人卡爾・桑德堡

山有蕨薇 / My Twitter Tiny Little Poems

Poetry is an echo,
asking a shadow to dance.

~ Carl Sandburg

卷末語

開始寫自以為是的短詩，是受到網路上幾位文友的啟迪。這當然沒有古代文人彼此答酬唱和的那種經典風範，只是一種不吐不快的感覺，某種知音之間的含蓄溝通，或者應該說是受到魯班影響而自己製造出來的幾把拙劣的斧頭。比方說下面這位專門在推特上創作短詩的凱特 (Katie Keys : Poet, @tinylittlepoem)；左邊是她的詩，右邊是我的應和：

我們觀察 　　於是看見 全世界 在文字裡。	我們航行 　　於是碇泊 全世界 在夢境裡。

再來便是文筆極為精鍊而充滿哲思的網友約翰・曼瑟爾 (John Mansell, @JohnMansell)，我第一次看到他的詩便十分喜歡，靈感大發。例如下面這首，左邊是約翰的詩，右邊是我的應和：

我不認識妳， 可能也永遠無緣。 然而在那瞬間， 妳在街上經過 我想到的只有妳。	雲彩飄過晴空， 轉瞬即逝。 然而在那瞬間， 雲影掠過湖面 湖水也為之蕩漾。

山有蕨薇 / My Twitter Tiny Little Poems

Author's Note

Three of my friends on Twitter inspired me into creating what I hope can be considered as poetry. Obviously I still have a lot to learn, as already demonstrated in this book. Very often it is just a subtle but naive response to certain words that touched me, a feeling I had to let out, an attempt to grab something beautiful and precious before it is gone. It began with this poem by "Katie Keys : Poet" (@tinylittlepoem) on the left, with my response on the right:

We observe,
   we see
the world
in words.
	We sail,
	   we anchor
	the world
	in dreams.

Then it was John Mansell (@JohnMansell), whose poems became my favourite since the very beginning:

I do not know you, and guess I never will. But for a second as you passed me in the street I thought of no one else.	The cloud drifts by, and is soon gone. Yet for a moment as its shadow touches the lake the water quivers.

接下來又回應了約翰的一首小詩：

我撲入妳的七彩，　　　　　他長身直入，
用我的身體作盤，　　　　　斑斕的色彩浪潮
進行調色。　　　　　　　　湧沒我今晚的月。

在這之後便不敢繼續應和了，以免有網路騷擾之嫌。事實上，我自己也驚訝於自己對情詩的愛好，也許是因為詩歌自古以來的功能就是吟詠情感，詩教溫柔敦厚，詩風秀麗清雅，所謂「感時花濺淚，恨別鳥驚心」一類的憂國傷世其實都是後來的流變。

　　如果是這樣，那麼我回應網友布萊恩·派垂克·郝利 (Brian Patrick Howley, @howleybrianp1) 的這首詩是否也有感懷世事的意味？

意念受感官啟迪　　　　　新的國度充滿行動
從心靈移民至　　　　　　舊的國度冰封加框。
　手上　　　　　　　　　移民：回憶和夢想
　紙上　　　　　　　　　之間的陰陽魔界。

人們追求新的感受
從國度移民至
　嶄新的國度

從這首詩開始，許多作品都是對於日常生活中所見所聞的感觸，轉化成象徵和符號的語言，試圖以詩歌的方式表達。我思索了許久，是否應該說明這些刻骨銘心的感觸究竟來源如何，讓我想到

山有蕨薇 / My Twitter Tiny Little Poems

Later I responded to another of John's poems:

I swept into your colours.	On it came
And mixed them on the palette	A splendid tide of colours
of my body.	submerged my moon tonight

The way I enjoy writing love poems is a surprise. Perhaps this is because since the beginning of time, songs and poems have been employed to express strong emotions. It was only later that poetry became a form of commentary. One example is my response to the following poem by Brian Patrick Howley (@howleybrianp1) is also a kind of social commentary:

Ideas inspired by senses   In the new lands are actions
Migrate from mind   with old lands frozen and framed.
  To hand   Migrants: The Twilight Zone
  To paper   between memories and dreams.

People aspiring to new sensation
Migrate from lands
  To Lands Anew.

Indeed, many of the poems collected here are my reflections on the events that took place throughout the writing of this book. I thought long and hard whether some of the what's and why's should be elaborated, in an attempt to help explain the subtle but wonderful

哪些譬喻，創作過程中又因為哪些明顯或微妙的轉折發生而可能讓讀者興發心有靈犀或搖頭苦笑的反應。然而，這樣的說明只是一種畫蛇添足吧。文字本身就是美，一如生活。生命的美好和悲涼只有自己能深切體會，如果說白就沒意思了。

總之，千言萬語，盡在不言中。希望你喜歡這本小書和它的雙語展現形式。今後如果有新作，當再和你分享。

process in which inspiration may be transformed into poetic writing Then I realised doing so would only "add feet to a snake", as the Chinese saying goes. After all, poetry itself, like life, is beauty. It cannot and should not be rationalised..

    I hope you enjoy this little bilingual book of poetry. I shall see you again some time in the future..

關於作者

孫運瑜生於台灣，現居澳洲墨爾本市，是中英雙語作家、翻譯、讀者、論者、自由記者和獨立學者。透過「電書朝代中文電子書店」，她協助新進和知名的英文作者、文學經紀人和出版社，將作品翻譯出版成電子書和紙本書，推廣到中文世界；與此同時，她也協助中文作家將作品推廣到英文世界。

About This Author

Born in Taiwan and now based in Melbourne, Australia, Christine Yunn-Yu Sun is a bilingual writer, translator, reader, reviewer, occasional journalist and independent scholar. Via eBook Dynasty, Christine assists emerging and established English-language authors, literary agents and publishers to translate, publish and promote their titles as ebooks and print books to the Chinese World, while helping Chinese-language authors promote their writings to the English World.

www.ingramcontent.com/pod-product-compliance
Lightning Source LLC
Chambersburg PA
CBHW071318080526
44587CB00018B/3271